MW01166563

MIXTAPES

Poetry By

Rachael Crosbie

Copyright © 2021 Rachael Crosbie
Copyright © 2021 Cover Design by Rachael Crosbie
Cover Font Licensing Credit to Vic Fieger License v1.00

ELJ Editions, Ltd. ~ New York
Magpies Series

All rights reserved.

ISBN-13: 978-1-942004-31-8

Praise for *MIXTAPES*

MIXTAPES shows us the connections between memories and dreams and nightmares like no other collection of poetry I have ever read. This collection does not hesitate to push boundaries and break expectations. Ambitious, daring and human. Rachael Crosbie has outdone herself.

— Tristan Cody, Creative Director of *POCKETFIRE*

Rachael Crosbie's *MIXTAPES* is a melodic dichotomy. In side 1, Crosbie frames the past self as a "you" in absentia, elegizing them at a distance, while her B-sides take a wistful turn toward a world where one's self is all there is. On both sides of this titular tape, lyrical, visceral visions will strike a chord with every reader. Long after reading, Crosbie's *MIXTAPES* will play on in your mind and heart.

— Isaura Ren, editor-in-chief of *perhappened* and author of *interlucent* (2020)

Aptly named, editor, songwriter, and poet Rachael Crosbie's collection, *MIXTAPES*, is a marriage of poetry and musical lyricism. Side 1: You in Absentia and Side 2: The B-Sides, though different, are two halves of a whole. Like a cassette loaded with precise and powerful imagery, each poem clicks into the next seamlessly. The speaker crones to the reader with each poem painting a picture of emotional yet tender. In a voice completely her own, Crosbie calls on the universal and is able to do something almost impossible: shape unrelenting emotion into unique, beautiful, melancholic language.

— Keana Aguila Labra, editor-in-chief of *Marías at Sampaguitas* and author of *NO SAINTS* (2020)

Acknowledgements

Thank you for all the late nights and confirmations – Shawn White, Tristan Cody, Keana Aguila Labra, and Rami Obeid, who have helped bring this book to life. Thank you to all who have supported my writing throughout the years and inspired me to never stop – Brandon Swarrow, Amy Randolph, Jill Sunday, Jamie Dessart, Melissa Martini, Kayla Kazarick, Abigail Bailey, Shawn White, and Tristan Cody. Thank you to a poetry class I took in my junior year of college and how it made me strive to push myself creatively. Thank you to my cats—Cosmo, Skitty, and Cuties—who reminded me that sleep and breaks are crucial. Thank you to my staff, past and present, on *the winnow magazine*, who are the most welcoming and reassuring people I've ever met. Thank you to my family who, somehow, knew I'd be a writer someday. Most importantly of all, thank you, dear reader for your careful and kind eye.

to those who feel burdened by the grief that comes with bad dreams, relationships, and friends.

•

SIDE 1:

YOU IN ABSENTIA

Contents

TW: sexual abuse, alcohol, bad dreams,

relationships, and friends

supercuts in absentia

conceived in staccato / supercuts, sutured memory only a
seer sees for another / you hiked to a dream punctuated with
/ things you never knew, bewitched / and haunted by light,
the kind / in the supermarket close / to home, blistering /
and tender and stark, the kind you / didn't mean to find. you
hiked / to a dream punctured by / a reminder: "you spend
too much time / in your mind."

doppelgänger in absentia

how did you sleep, peach slipping from skin / to astral shades. how did you sleep, chasing memories / sparklers on the beach awashed / with honey-color leaking / through dark, / sharp magenta, pain you catalogued / in your sleep / you, a child / jagged with rabid dreams and pleading / nosebleeds, predicting / a slinky banshee / screeched static / screens blank with grief / everything lost from exposure / forgotten fairytales / exorcisms for children. / you searched for a mirrored realm / a doppelgänger dimension / where you didn't need / the same existence.

she read you like tarot, a threat / she claimed to be possessed, / seeing through a planchette / the planned trance, a bit / voyeur, a bit for her, she / broke you with imitations / of the dead, she / said nightmare or forced / recall, truth or dare. she / wanted touch, movement ritual / to adults and refusal / would turn to fault. she read / from obituaries and promised / proof through a makeshift / séance with your body / dizzied in youth, and you, / a pawn for tricks, / arranged psychic partitions.

you projected here last time / you slept, conquered by / the ghoulish daze / when you chased after dreams / disguised by arthouse horror and / pixelated violations. / consider the curse of memory that / refused to stay in the periphery, that / clawed out medieval and raw / like when you cut / yourself with mirrors / broken by hand, broken for / modern bloodletting / or when / you saw the dead in reflections / at dawn / where twilight bled grief-ruined and / thieved you of feeling. / you projected here last / time you slept, conquered by / poltergeists tarantulated / into the trauma priming you / for unkind appraisal. / you were handled / by older others who glitched / with predatory magic / who made you beg / to physically dissociate.

the shock of daylight beamed / through a window, a dream / where you learned to love / barefoot in beachwater / the sky slanted / with apricot and oil / or a bloodbath / where the periphery loosened / a staircase peppered with summer dusk / haunting from that window / sand shifting to shag carpet / waves to ripples of weak air-conditioning / this basement shook your vision / the basement trembling and viscous / the basement where you had sex for the first time, where / you thought that was sex, his flesh / and voice quivering / when you projected out / to somewhere else.

laying in a hammock, a loose / womb of yarn and air, / safe where you played / pretend, tethered to warmth, / tethered to stillborn / rapport from others. / you mimicked movies / alone where final girls / escaped mystic warnings / in the shape of / a troubled hitchhiker with a switchblade and twitching with your Polaroids / double-vision pirouetting like bodies animated by the visceral blaze of night / a part that you played with a wreath of breathing blooms and brief sacrifice, / all what grieved you of clarity. / these seething cuts / marred by mirage / some kind of sleep deprived / you to starve / the proof of sensory abuse / seducing you / to reprise the role / from your childhood.

anesthesia in absentia

a glimpse into the absence / where skies wheeled limp and counterfeit, / a fuzzy white you wanted to cleave / you tried to hold, to press / into a notebook, pressing / blankness from wishes you whispered / to dead relatives, to missed memories you / buried into paper, into pink coffins / into the division of here and there / into la petite mort, where / electronic fissures exhumed you / with superficial light and / traveled you back to where / you were afraid / of the body manifesting you and you / manifesting in the body. / fevered fits shifted sweat to sickness / trapping you in this loop / where you woke up confused, choking / on a room cleaved by white.

insomnia in absentia

sifting through some shadowbox with sand, some /
displaced sentimentality scalped you, some / time in Texas
you breathed in a sallow sun / morning, wanting some / one.
the dry glow slaughters the moment with / stitchings of
insomnia. you project one good / thing onto the miasma of
/ matches, swiping right until the next midnight / thawed,
loosening to soft smoke, to / when you swear ghosts appear
to / almost warm / austere of unknowns.

timber and sagebrush blaze / quick and white / in the quiet
dark / burns like when you drank / Russian vodka straight /
and alone. in the morning, / you crushed an egg / slurring
shell and yoke / with a migraine. / your hand pressed /
against an open oven, / craving that blaze. / even in winter
/ sleet and embers bleed, / glazing over to black and rock
salt. / when you jumped out of a moving car, / to brackish
asphalt hues, / the cold crackled too.

wool weather infused with musk / smoke, subconscious humidity / glazing like sweat in your eyes / when you arrived / to your Chinatown room swathed in / warm salmon light, in / dusk dissected by the bleating / of pigeons and / pruning introspection. / another day, you'd let yourself get lost / in a puckered haze, simulated / by the hissing of scalding showers / safe with static, and / you won't sleep, you'll / slink to the balcony / seeking out amnesia.

euphoria in absentia

___

the day shed / in swathes of peplum purple dark, threads / settling in your wraith-blonde hair, / tethered like dancers / in an awkward waltz. / your footing swayed to a daze of pixelated night, to / a blaze of neon wire, to / a gaze unknown / that stuck with you / a kind of déjà vu wrinkled / when you'd dream / in periwinkle, whispers, / anything etched in light.

About the Author

Rachael Crosbie is from a small town outside of Pittsburgh, Pennsylvania. She has a BA in English Literature, and she is currently studying Publishing at New York University: School of Professional Studies. Rachael is the Editor-in-Chief and founder of *the winnow magazine*, the Poetry Editor of *POCKETFIRE*, and a poetry reader for *Persephone's Daughters*. You can find her poetry in *Re-Side*, *Cobra Milk*, *Lucky Pierre Zine*, and others. She's probably tweeting about cats, *The Haunting of Bly Manor*, and poetry at @rachaelapoet.

MIXTAPES

Poetry By

Rachael Crosbie

Copyright © 2021 Rachael Crosbie
Copyright © 2021 Cover Design by Rachael Crosbie
Cover Font Licensing Credit to Vic Fieger License v1.00

ELJ Editions, Ltd. ~ New York
Magpies Series

All rights reserved.

ISBN-13: 978-1-942004-31-8

Praise for *MIXTAPES*

MIXTAPES shows us the connections between memories and dreams and nightmares like no other collection of poetry I have ever read. This collection does not hesitate to push boundaries and break expectations. Ambitious, daring and human. Rachael Crosbie has outdone herself.

— Tristan Cody, Creative Director of *POCKETFIRE*

Rachael Crosbie's *MIXTAPES* is a melodic dichotomy. In side 1, Crosbie frames the past self as a "you" in absentia, elegizing them at a distance, while her B-sides take a wistful turn toward a world where one's self is all there is. On both sides of this titular tape, lyrical, visceral visions will strike a chord with every reader. Long after reading, Crosbie's *MIXTAPES* will play on in your mind and heart.

— Isaura Ren, editor-in-chief of *perhappened* and author of *interlucent* (2020)

Aptly named, editor, songwriter, and poet Rachael Crosbie's collection, *MIXTAPES*, is a marriage of poetry and musical lyricism. Side 1: You in Absentia and Side 2: The B-Sides, though different, are two halves of a whole. Like a cassette loaded with precise and powerful imagery, each poem clicks into the next seamlessly. The speaker crones to the reader with each poem painting a picture of emotional yet tender. In a voice completely her own, Crosbie calls on the universal and is able to do something almost impossible: shape unrelenting emotion into unique, beautiful, melancholic language.

— Keana Aguila Labra, editor-in-chief of *Marías at Sampaguitas* and author of *NO SAINTS* (2020)

Acknowledgements

The author gratefully acknowledges the editors of the following publications where these poems first appeared:

Cobra Milk, "Where All Your Nightmares Converge; *Muse & Stone*, "Spotify Playlist 2018: How to Start a Séance on Loop" and "Saudade, for when you're gone"; *Off the Coast*, "Lipstick & Fish"; *Pussy Magic*, "Camouflage Tethered"; and *Sigma Tau Delta Rectangle*, "Crocodile in the Bathtub."

Thank you for all the late nights and confirmations – Shawn White, Tristan Cody, Keana Aguila Labra, and Rami Obeid, who have helped bring this book to life. Thank you to all who have supported my writing throughout the years and inspired me to never stop – Brandon Swarrow, Amy Randolph, Jill Sunday, Jamie Dessart, Melissa Martini, Kayla Kazarick, Abigail Bailey, Shawn White, and Tristan Cody. Thank you to a poetry class I took in my junior year of college and how it made me strive to push myself creatively. Thank you to my cats—Cosmo, Skitty, and Cuties—who reminded me that sleep and breaks are crucial. Thank you to my staff, past and present, on *the winnow magazine*, who are the most welcoming and reassuring people I've ever met. Thank you to my family who, somehow, knew I'd be a writer someday. Most importantly of all, thank you, dear reader for your careful and kind eye.

to those who feel burdened by the grief that comes with
bad dreams, relationships, and friends.

SIDE 2:

THE B-SIDES

Contents

TW: sexual abuse, alcohol, bad dreams,

relationships, and friends

Spotify Playlist 2018:
How to Start a Séance on Loop

Prisms cut through vision, warm / and flickering. Soon the afterglow / was jettisoned by dusk, and I followed / you. I believed we were exiles, wandering / into the curious nighttime. We weren't. / I crossed through patches where the moon / didn't touch, crossed through a low breeze / stitched in strands of reeds, crossed over / it all / for you.

You promised me the end of the hike, / and I followed you, stumbling / in the wrong path, in the wrong night. / You promised me things / that didn't belong to you, to this world, / when spurs were stinging through the dark fabric of my jeans. / Prisms cut through my vision, and you / vanished with the sunrise.

Lipstick & Fish

She shaved the patch above of her vulva when she was ten. A pink Gillette dulled by her mother. When slippery, it dragged skin. Shock mauled her nerves. Dropping the razor, water washed it to the drain. Water washed with light pink. She thought about her period: tampons dispensed in the mall, *American Girl Doll Guide to Puberty*, her mother's lipstick smeared up to her cheeks. She told me. But I was not a woman. A girl as she was. My body sprouted sparse hairs and raw pink buds. She pulled down my roller-skate patterned panties and held a mirror to my vagina. Spread by my fingers, it opened like the gutted belly of a fish. Exposed to the tampon in close range, in her hand.

Strange Magic

From a silk sky, dusk bled / snow splitting my hands / into ribbons / like the strange magic / that fingered / my corrugated hair, that dragged / my panties to a wrinkle of pink pastels, that / dissected me when I was unwilling, / the magic put into words / by someone else.

I plunged my knuckles bare / into winter, to the crisp dirt / awash with blood, / my skin raw and sheared / to threads, I walked / to a fire that won't exist.

Crocodile in the Bathtub

I don't know how I got here, coughing up coarse air by the lake. A dying sun haloed copper on my hair.

Black rushed through and reflected ripples in water, reaching the patch of dirt and grass where I sat cross-legged and numb from the damp earth. I left and let my body walk me to selfishly spilled trash, mistaken for a gutted crocodile, laying on the street—walk me to a parking lot buzzing with people. I followed them.

I followed them to mint hydrangeas—plastic still sheathing—and kneeled before the dead, too. I whispered a goodbye to him, signed my name in the guest book, and dipped my fingers in the water cased in gold leaves and coins. I didn't know him.

I wake up cold in the bathtub, water splattering on the tile when dawn projects in my motel room, and peach plunges back in my skin.

I don't know how I got here.

Birthday in Tableau

Squirrels bury acorns in the now
threadbare daffodil sweater, fuzzy and warm.

They bury acorns where it laid abandoned—
stuck in May 2008 with bonfires that were sheltered

by child chalk designs and glacial company,
the shadows I make
with my hands onto the pavement:
rabbits that won't run, wolves that won't chase.
Pure halcyon, grace.

Stuck in May 2008 when I'm talking about
the dead replacing today
when I've moved to another May, another decade,
another birthday. Here, there is a frozen
long island to commemorate,

a breakup. Dizzied and frayed, I stumbled
to the parking lot alone,
holding onto the dead.

Camouflage.Tethered

A dream about nighttime:

> country roads fissured by rain. electronic
> waters that won't slip through fingers.
> mirrors in a bedroom sheltered
> by husky darkness, camouflage. I searched
> for the coordinates to these places I've
> never been,
> the reflection.

But dawn broke through loose stitching in curtains that
were hand-sewn by a relative from the east who believes
dreams exist to haunt us but don't mean anything.

She held the door open to her trailer deluged
in the jazz song that conceived her.
And she pointed me toward the spare room—
the windows   bare, tethered to night,
and the bed   hidden by a hoard of mirrors.

Saudade, for when you're gone

Snow peppered the sky, reminding me
of crinkled foil, leftovers. I rinsed my hands
in the sink—the one where if the cool lights
strike it right, the sink turns
to a silver gradient.
Outside my kitchen window, this tangible gray
offered the absence of things.

I searched everywhere for quarters,
to call you from the laundromat. You never answered.
So, I drove to the white sands,
wind howling with specks of cold water.

I walked barefoot in the dark,
dead sparklers—shaped into thorns—
splintered my skin. Visitors always treat the beach
like they were celebrating July.

I continued toward the shore.
The ocean blackened the further it went on,
and the rising waves abridged the difference
in color between the water and sky.

I wandered closer to the dock—
the one that will soon be demolished.
The wind slipped through my body,
dizzying and visceral.
I saw you here some night, some dream,
and I shuffled my numb feet in the sand, waiting.
Waiting to understand how to find you here,
at this dock,
at this beach.

Looking for Directions in Two Parts

Your orange cat swiped coins
that glinted in sunlight. We knew
this went on for hours, but we left
that winter afternoon, driving
to our reservation. Two minutes out,
we seemed to materialize
in our car, spinning
on the roads too calloused by snow.
And we laughed until vision divided
like a kaleidoscope, we laughed while we waited
for the snowplow, for the clearing.

You parked the Corolla by the whiteshuttered ranch
and left my jacket in the shape of a black saucer
on the porch you hesitated
for a moment, a phantom touch from the last
night slipping from your hands.
A glimpse of rabbit twitched
in the background, in the field behind you,
pulling toward your car. You thumbed the leather
of your seat like a newborn
as you settled in and drove on.

Beach Vacation, 2019

The last night reimagined as a vacation—
losing you
at dinner where we only drank expensive wine
and folded napkins into barricades.

We sat across from each other, forgetting how to talk.
When you left, walking into dusk, the distance buzzed.
I wanted to chase after you like a wolf—
a primal wish for your physical body to be here
again, but I didn't.

I woke up on the beach, my fingers sinking into silk sand
as waves drifted closer. I convinced myself
that the last night was a bad dream. When dawn sliced
through a dizzying sky, I turned
into a child, caught up in cotton vision and magic,
the sandcastle shifted to a clay hut
and stood in that morning fog—the dark speck wavering
in wind, in beige weather.

Where All My Nightmares Converge

Sometimes I sleep on a mountain where the warm sun
reflects copper on my hair, and a light wind pulls strands in
the direction where lichen grows in patches near ribbons of
water and snake-sloughed-skin—marbled with moon and
old dollar bills. It could be the stitching of my leather jacket
unworn, and there is a shadow of a poacher in my black
jacket lining—shots fire in the distance, muted by powder
and smoke. Still I dream.

Sometimes I sleep on a wooden boat where I'm a
fisherman with cheeks marked by broken blood vessels that
resemble spider legs, and the low pulse of wind textured by
sleet. Water underneath sloshes like a jar of aged peaches,
and I reel in dead fish—my bait twined with anti-freeze.
The skin on my lips pulls apart when I fillet fish with my
pocketknife. I know the risk—too metallic and harsh and
the subconscious craving. Still I dream.

Sometimes I sleep, denying who I am and still I dream.

On Navigation

I wanted a house sliced with hidden rooms—corridors
spliced by faint electricity, cool pastels shifting with every
movement, memories from an unknown period of time.
You'd tell me that this was a metaphor for something, that
I'm using unfamiliar territory as a barrier for what I never
want to uncover. Did you ever consider that I was tired of
living in an apartment smaller than most trailers? One
where each door was visible when I walk in, where we hid
from each other, where I can see my entire history from the
past six months?

You never moved in. Not when I begged. Not when the
lease was up, and my roommate decided the city was too
dangerous to live in. You assured me that you weren't ready
for such an undertaking, living so far from school. Then
why did you move in with these people, these strangers
you'd only known for what felt like a minute of time? I
could only imagine that you must be so used to me that I
was something dispensable, boring, or known.

Even if things were different, and I had the money, you
wouldn't move in with me. Not even if I found a house in
the country with a landscape of lush nowhere and nighttime
visits from raccoons and coyotes. You love animals, even
the ones that might be a little rabid, a little too predatory to
be loved. You gave your love so easily to everything and
everyone else.

Late October, we went to parties. You got drunk on a haze of lights, dancing. You didn't ask me to join. You left me at the bar, and someone else took your seat. You weren't bothered; you were among friends. I was an accessory that you leave at the table and don't think twice if someone swipes it. The music blazed, the ice softened in my glass, and you were dancing with your friends, kissing them, even—why didn't I worry then?

I went back alone. I navigated the blistering dark, looking behind myself after every block. Not for you. When I made it to the subway station, the air stitched by cold nights, I waited. I tossed memories into the barren track and listened for the screeching of the 6 train. It rushed by, empty, blurring yellow ground. Twenty more minutes to speculate, to readjust, to speculate, to readjust, to mutilate my emotions to where I was torn between myself and you. And I always chose you.

About the Author

Rachael Crosbie is from a small town outside of Pittsburgh, Pennsylvania. She has a BA in English Literature, and she is currently studying Publishing at New York University: School of Professional Studies. Rachael is the Editor-in-Chief and founder of *the winnow magazine*, the Poetry Editor of *POCKETFIRE*, and a poetry reader for *Persephone's Daughters*. You can find her poetry in *Re-Side*, *Cobra Milk*, *Lucky Pierre Zine*, and others. She's probably tweeting about cats, *The Haunting of Bly Manor*, and poetry at @rachaelapoet.